Moments of Time

Mark Fleisher

Moments of Time

Mercury HeartLink
www.heartlink.com

Contents

BACKWARD GLANCES

NOTIONS OF LOVE

A la Carte

Random Samples I

Random Samples II

Epilogue

Moments of Time

Merle

For believing in me

Kate

You fought the good fight

Claire, Abby, Ella

Keeping the flame burning

"In science one tries to tell people, in such a way as to be understood by everyone, something that no one ever knew before. But in poetry, it's the exact opposite."

—Paul Dirac (1902-1984)
1933 Nobel Prize recipient in physics

"Who am I? I am a poet.
What do you do? I write.
How do I live? I live."

Rodolfo, Act I of Giacomo Puccini's opera *La Boheme*

Acknowledgments

An affair of the heart brought me to Albuquerque permanently in October 2013 after three years of "commuting" from the Finger Lakes area of New York. Believe me when I say Southwest Airlines and I became good friends during those three years.

The wonderful woman who honors me with her love has first dibs on my heart. Next come the people, culture, and natural beauty of the Land of Enchantment.

I became attracted to writing poetry late in life. My early efforts seem amateurish and naive. After extensive editing and rewriting, some of those poems appear in this volume. If I have achieved any proficiency as a poet, I must thank any number of people, beginning with the diverse and talented Albuquerque-area poetry community for the warm welcome into their ranks. Untold thanks to Billy Brown and Bill Nevins for giving me opportunities to read my poetry, and for their support and encouragement. The baby steps I took as a writer of poetry lengthened their stride thanks to Jules Nyquist and her "Food as a Metaphor" workshop.

Thanks to Melony Benassi, my Kentucky amiga, for insisting that I did have a book somewhere inside of me; and to Chris Denton in Elmira, NY, perhaps the only attorney-poet-hockey player in the galaxy, who generously shared his exquisite writings while often neglecting to bill me for legal services.

Very special thanks to Patrick Houlihan, poet, professor, musician, and mentor. I enrolled in Patrick's

Creative Writing:Poetry class at Central New Mexico Community College in the 2014 summer session. Sitting in a classroom for the first time in 50 years gave me the jitters. Thanks to Patrick, my experience was college without the angst. Reading, studying, and analyzing poetry and poetic forms contributed so much to my growth.

In October 2010, I reconnected with Merle Pokempner, now my partner, soulmate, and best friend. Her love, caring, and sense of humor light the paths of change I continue to travel. A woman of incredible courage and integrity, she brings out whatever good qualities I might possess while keeping me grounded. Thank you for your inspiration and for putting up with my quirks and idiosyncrasies.

Mark Fleisher
Albuquerque, NM

PROLOGUE

I Am...

I am a complexity, a contradiction, a complication
I am your daily planner
I am spontaneously combusted by existential forces
I am a risk taker, courting catastrophe
I am unafraid to disconnect from the know
I am unafraid of unfamiliar landscapes
I am shielded from the curious by panes thick with frost
I am entered by the chosen through permitted transparencies
I am witness to the sting of tumultuous death
I am mindful of a quiet passing
I am mourning all in God's design
I am a minnow in a school of swimmers speaking alien languages
I am walking only in my tracks
I am No Man
I am Every Man.

QUIETUDE

OCEAN GIFTS

A beach is but a beach
when eyes see only expanses
of sand and water.
A beach is more when
rocks jaggedly carved
and whittled by infinite waves
millennium after millennium
rise from the crashing tide.
A beach is more
when stone cliffs
plunge to the sea;
when headlands majestically
oversee their domain;
when winged sentinels
remain silent except
for warning alarms
should interlopers
disturb their roost.

What did the eye see
10,000 years before?
What may the eye see
10,000 years ahead?

A generation past,
a loved one since taken.
Now the water suctions
remorse and regret
from the soul, transfusing
renewal and rebirth

into welcoming veins,
lubricating heartstrings,
nourishing memory.
Loving once more,
breathing anew
when a beach is more
than a beach.

Mountain Time

A river rushes,
A bird calls,
A zephyr sings.

Who seeks answers
finds truth reigning
in a paradise crowned by
a dollop of heaven.
Stand on tip-toes,
stretch skyward,
imagine leaving
fingerprints engraved
on blue palettes.
Unhurried clouds
drift aimlessly
toward undetermined
ports of call.

A river rushes,
A bird calls,
A zephyr sings.

A New Way of Walking

What do I miss during exercise for exercise's sake?
On a treadmill electronic glare and blare enter my zone,
not browns, blacks, whites, men, women, muscular, spindly.
Left-right, left-right, left-right, left-right, about face,
left-right, left-right, left-right, left-right
along the Rio Grande ditch,
rarely seeing, sensing, smelling, hearing, touching.

Not this morning when pink and white English primroses
peek from weedy growth, wild flowers glorify chicken wire,
mallards glide gracefully through the murky brown,
slowing to nuzzle beaks like newly-minted lovers.

I clear sleep's residue from eyes' corners,
turning my landscape from a blurry Monet to
the sharp features of a Bierstadt mountain.

I avoid slippery, slimy, smelly dung dumped
on camel-colored paths flanking
this murky rill made by man for man.

A more mannerly horse - a chestnut - her measured
gait's clip-clop leaving faint evidence; pony tails
of mount and rider swaying as matched pendulums.

Among the meager collection of walkers
only a stone-faced woman resembling our tyrannical
grade school teacher ignores my "good morning."
I hear mental "tut-tuts" as I scribble my impressions.

Warbled reprises of reveille compete
with raspy howls from the throats
of unseen creatures of unknown breeds
screened by splintered fences.

Strolling amid the dapple of sunshine
and shadow, I meet baby lizards darting
from ground cover to ground cover, and a
roadrunner showing off its State Bird status.

Gnarled as unshelled walnuts, natural hollows
in decaying trees, reminders of dried out faces
of weathered cowpokes, prematurely
aged by whipping winds and baking suns.

Walking comes with warnings:
Beware of Dog, No Trespassing,
No Parking, Private Property.
Finally, a friendly
Honey for Sale,
Call 505-344-9747,
What to think? Direct line to the bees?

Moving Along

Glide across Kentucky, flow smoothly
into the verdant hills and hollows
caressing West Virginia's arteries.

Wonderful names -- Hurricane,
Nitro, Mink Shoals, Big Otter, Big Sandy River,
too many bridges memorializing
too many privates, corporals, sergeants.

Country music the radio's main course,
one station's constant twang replacing
another's strains of family, religion,
unrequited love drifting to the ether.

I love again, praying I may keep it so,
honor her time and space, or risk
a parting of her choice, but my fault.

Could I walk away, nonchalant and composed?
I fool no one, only a lie to think I might dismiss
the last love I know
for I shall not command my heart to seek another.

Silent Night

Winter night
stars still,
moon silent,
wind hushed.
Hear snowflakes
fall on frozen ground -
  almost.

Tracks of rabbits,
deer, maybe coyote,
embedded without a whisper
on white blankets.
Window panes opaque
with coats of stealthy frost.
All sound suspended
in midnight chill.

Vertical No More

There's a tree in my yard
no longer vertical,
uprooted clean as a whistle,
looks almost surgical.

Gusts from Miss Sandy
so violent, fanatical,
from this ghastly weather
I need a sabbatical.

BEST TIMES

Walk along alabaster sand,
stride for stride, hand-in-hand,
glean an opalescent shell from shore,
listen to the waves' melodic roar.

Watch the golden circle of sun
proclaim this glorious day is done,
regally slip into the sea,
a private twilight for you and me.

CYCLE OF SEVEN

Come 7 I look East where fog drapes itself
    upon every crest, crag and arete
At mid-morning, the mist burns into
    quiet oblivion
Exposing jagged rock stretching high
    above the imaginary sea
Mounds of mashed potatoes masquerading as clouds
    pockmark blue sky
Silver-sided behemoths choreograph
    intersecting vapor trails
Exclamation points soon fade
    into the ether
Others seem on a collision course
    though safely separated by space
Come 7 I look East when the departing sun splashes
    crimson strokes upon an irregular canvas.
These mountains answer to Sandia -
    watermelon in Spanish.
Bien Mur — big mountain
    say the ancients.

A New Mexico Haiku

A grasshopper flits
the roadrunner thrusts its tongue
Breakfast is served

My Haven

Engines power down as well-honed blades
slice through final blades of grass;
yelping dogs only whimper now;
infants sleep under blue and pink protectors.

I pass this quiet time with pages illuminated
by a soft glow, though welcome thoughts
dwelling in my heart and feeding the soul
erase the gulf of geography I must span.

Unseen tenants of the night croak and chirp,
a train whistle calls out to unknown riders.
As I strain to hear your voice in my head,
a voice confidently answered out loud,
believing my words reach you through
a connection I feel but cannot yet describe.

My head tilts toward stars in the blackness
filling a skylight's rectangle, reminding
me of silent walks under your night's
supply of heavenly lights.
Tomorrow night and the next,
this solitary reverie until we marvel
together under the same sky, the same stars.

TURBULENCE

A War Haiku

Fragments of metal
invading his innocence
He comes home too soon

Red Dust

On my face, in my ears,
up my nostrils,
only goggles shield my eyes.
Welcome to Song Be,
and Red Dust and
Operation Eagle Thrust.
Red dust swirling in
prop wash of Caribous and Providers
whose pilots skillfully
negotiate a too short runway,
lifting off, loaded
with fresh-faced troops,
their tickets punched
for the next performance
of this theater of the absurd.

And me, weighted by notebooks, cameras,
recording all this for someone's posterity.
Me, a few months removed
from a second Cape summer
where I wore starched Class A's,
three stripes adorning each sleeve.
Pete, Surfer John, Jimmy Lee, me,
CC and ginger on payday nights,
hearing sweet-voiced Jan sing
even after we ended our fling.

Now in combat regalia,
a .38 holstered on my hip,
M-16 slung over a shoulder,

awake in bunkers each night,
protected from mortar shells
showered from VC perches
we abandon each night
and they forsake at dawn
in this game I call musical hilltops.

If there is a God, I will find
a long and steamy and
powerful shower to dissolve
Red Dust.
Not yet, God says,
I am stranded in Dalat,
cool in the mountains,
summer playground when
emperors ruled.
Palettes of lettuce bound
for the general's mess
bump me from my flight.
General's mess, oh yes.

I get my shower next day,
long and steamy and powerful,
scraping Red Dust from my tired self.
Red Dust gone,
the Red Dust I see,
not the sweet smell
of aviation gas
nor the acrid smell
of gunpowder,
Red Dust, the vision,
  all remain.

LUCKY MAN
(dedicated to Rick Ramsey)

Days to go -- two-o-eight --
until the sweet bird swoops and
plucks me from this
benighted place before
dark messengers intervene.

Rick the tease.
I am the short-timer! *
I am FIGMO! **
I am 18 days and a wake up, boys!
I am Lucky Man...
until an eerie whine
awakens ghosts, then
impulsively explodes,
sending rampaging shards
of red-hot shrapnel tumbling headlong.

Cascaded into terror,
ears concussed, eyes dust-filled,
spurting blood stipples my face,
splatters across my chest,
a cocktail for the dark messenger?
one for whose road? whose last call?

Lucky Man...until his lank body
shredded, sickeningly splayed about,
scooped into a black rubber cocoon.
Once the Lucky Man...now he is home
        too soon.

Grief and guilt whirl
in my mind's maelstrom,
unable to decipher
the impenetrable mystery
how bombs and rockets and
shells and bullets
name their victims.

Another Lucky Man tomorrow.
Not my tomorrow -- two-o-seven
if Lucky Man's mantle
drapes these shoulders.

* short-timer - someone having a very few days left in his/her tour of
   duty in Vietnam.
** FIGMO - An acronym for Fuck. I Got My Orders — orders for going
   home.

SHARED INGREDIENTS

January's final day 1968,
bullets whizz past my head
ricocheting off pavement,
imbedding in soft earth,
mortar rounds arc overhead
Happy New Year, G.I.
Up and down and across
this tortured land
unfriendlies shatter an
undeclared holiday truce.
A Saigon girl of 10
and her family seek shelter
from frightening barrages.

1975 — again she hides
after a soon-to-be disgraced
president satisfies a war-weary public
by proclaiming "peace with honor."
What peace? Whose honor?
She withstands 11 years
of harsh rule, fleeing
first by boat before finding this
landlocked haven.

Fast forward 46 Januaries,
nuoc mam's saltiness,
lemongrass' perfume,
lotus root's delicacy,
siricha's heat
now seduce my senses
on San Mateo Boulevard.

Not my place to ask
of those 11 years for fear
of recalling nightmares,
Instead, we embrace,
exchange New Year's wishes.
We may talk again of shared times,
shared thoughts of those defining days.

Maybe not.

FREEDOM FLIGHT

Friday the thirteenth,
lucky or not, I wonder,
clambering aboard my Pegasus.
thinking if others are aware.

We've spent our year,
some a few months longer,
a year shaking and shaping my world.
Tet — no need to say more;
a year when *"slain civil rights leader"*
enters the permanent vocabulary;
a year when a devil in the City of Angels
murders another heroic brother;
now remembered names emblazon
streets and schools and stadiums
they will never see.

A year when a tormented president whose
massive right hand once grasped mine
tells his divided nation,
*"I shall not seek and I will not accept
the nomination...for another term..."*

I return to nowhere, to no one,
better than somewhere, someone?
I belong only to me.

Friday the thirteenth,
keep the runway clear of craters,
free from a random rocket's havoc.
Quietly, slowly, push back,

navigate the labyrinth of concrete aisles,
wheeling to start position,
engines at max thrust, rpms climbing,
brakes released, we hurtle ahead,
five seconds, ten seconds, fifteen seconds,
"Hail Mary, full of grace..."
angling toward the blue vastness,
aloft in the dank air of late summer.

In a minute, an unseen voice,
"Ladies and gentlemen,
we have left the airspace
of South Vietnam."
A tsunami of cheers washes
 over all,
"Home my man. Back to the world."
Guam, Hawaii, finally California.
"The land of round eyes."
Friday the thirteenth — lucky day.
(Baruch ator adonai, eloheinu, melech ha'olom, hatou,
vhameitiu)
Blessed are you Ha Shem, our God, King of the Universe,
   the Good and Doer of Good.

Lucky Man II

Now Lucky Man,
lucky, alive,
finding best places
at worst times,
the wheel stops
beyond my number,
aces and eights
dealt to the unlucky ones.

Now Lucky Man,
lucky, alive
for the surgeon's
deft hand excises
messengers of mortality
hosting microscopic souvenirs
likely conceived
by renegade agents.

Now Lucky Man,
lucky, alive,
welcoming the morning's
first cup, hearing
soft footsteps padding about,
impossible had I
ventured elsewhere,
had the blade
been misdirected.

To End All Wars

You're of a certain age
I confidently say
if you remember
Armistice Day.

Recall a railroad car
somewhere in France
where generals
danced a verbal dance
to end the war
to end all wars
for sure.

Thousands of men
hurled into battle
prodded and pushed
like so many cattle.

Thousands bogged down
in dank, muddy trenches,
their nostrils inhaling
death's stinks and stenches.

Airplanes, tanks,
clouds of poison gas,
patriotic slogans shouting
"They Shall Not Pass."

Amid the pools of blood
mountains of gore,

did anyone ask
what's it all for?

Some whiskered archduke
got himself knocked off
an event perhaps worthy
of a second-rate cough.

Then an epidemic spread
an infection so viral
with nations whirling
into a suicidal spiral.

And when the Kaiser
sold his embittered soul
the fighting exacted
a horrible toll.

Yanks, Frenchmen, Germans,
Russians, so many Brits,
a generation lost
until they called it quits
to end the war
to end all wars
for sure.

THE UNKNOWN PRICE

For eight dollars and a few cents
I can buy Shoe Goo,
a compound of toluene, solvent naphtha,
to repair a sole flapping away
after divorcing from
the leather boot on my right foot.

Eight dollars and a few cents,
I think what if such a small amount
might repair not s-o-l-e-s, but s-o-u-l-s
returning from desert battles,
mountain conflicts, firefights in
teeming urban neighborhoods,
remote mud-hutted villages.
Souls in broken bodies or bodies
opaquely whole to the naked eye.
Titled people with strings
of letters following names
speak of moral injury,
unseen wounds inflicted,
undetected by medical machines.

A dark-skinned, dark-eyed
10-year-old brandishes a grenade,
a 20-year-old grunt shoots
        him dead,
the grenade falls to the ground,
        not exploding
but bouncing among other rocks,
the soldier hardened beyond his years,

hardened for all his days,
a damaged soul drowned in guilt.
    Moral Injury

Restoration upon their return?
        How? Where?
Rites of penitence, purification,
values, beliefs betrayed,
questioning motives of deities,
asking how gods allow such acts,
abandoned by higher powers.

Moral injury — What price?

BACKWARD GLANCES

GOTTA GET ME A BLACK TURTLENECK

Men reading their poetry
don't wear black turtlenecks —
at least not like another time.

Army fatigue jackets,
L.L. Bean hunting shirts, REI chic,
vests graced by Native American symbols,
none unexpected in New Mexico.
One fellow even wore a button down
white shirt accessorized by a striped tie.
No black turtlenecks in the house.

When we called presidents three-letter words,
high school hipsters read
Ferlinghetti, Ginsberg, Corso,
pretending they dug every word, every nuance,
Village tables encircled by true and imagined literati
sipping sugarless, creamless coffee, mesmerized
by turtlenecked, goateed, shades-wearing,
cool chic masters drawing smoky puffs
through tortoise-shell holders.
Hands unmet in praise and approval,
snapping fingers to applaud,
so very with it in 1950s NYC,
later discuss the sound of one hand clapping,
confronting this conundrum as scholars
might wrangle over arcane Talmudic passages.

Parading along Bleecker Street,
we disdainfully sidestep tourists from the heartland,

cameras dangling from their leathery necks,
legions of Hoosiers, Buckeyes, Gophers, Badgers, Hawkeyes,
straight from delis where laconic Jewish waiters
rolled their eyes while silently delivering
pastrami on soggy white bread
slathered and spread with Hellman's best.

We down underage beer at the testosterone turf
of McSorley's Old Ale House on East 7th,
next the White Horse on Hudson,
few years too late to eavesdrop
on the Original Dylan, for his last call
sounded in chilled darkness six weeks
before the Alban Arthan of 1953; *
wonder if he wore a black turtleneck
going gently or not into that good night.

I construct occasional lines,
reciting when connected to courage.
Gotta get me a black turtleneck, I think.

* Welsh for the Light of Winter; i.e. Winter Solstice.

October Trilogy

Growing up in the Brooklyn, New York, of the 1940s and 1950s meant my love and loyalty were with the Dodgers. The "Boys of Summer" of Roger Kahn's book of the same name were my heroes. "Dem Bums" as they were affectionately called could raise your spirits, then break your heart — all in the same baseball season. That feature led to the title of my unfinished and barely started boyhood memoir titled "I Died Twice Before Age 15."

My initial demise came in 1951 when the Dodgers faced the archrival New York Giants in a best-of-three playoff for the National League pennant and the right to reach the World Series. The teams were tied one game apiece after the Dodgers blew a 13-game lead during the regular season. Brooklyn led the Giants 4-1 entering the ninth inning of the deciding playoff game. New York scored once, then off the bat of Bobby Thomson — "The Flying Scot" — came "The Shot Heard 'Round the World," a three-run walk-off home run to send me and the Borough of Brooklyn into dark despair.

Resurrection, albeit temporary, came four years later when the Dodgers defeated the New York Yankees for their first and only World Series championship in Brooklyn. A stunning catch by Sandy Amoros and the brilliant pitching of young left hander Johnny Podres clinched the seventh and deciding game, triggering a tumultuous celebration among the faithful.

The revelry lasted two more seasons before Dodgers' owner Walter O'Malley delivered the coup de grace. On October 8, 1957, he announced the abandonment of Brooklyn for the Left Coast, specifically a stadium near the La Brea Tar Pits of Los Angeles. The

Boys of Summer — My Boys of Summer — headed to LaLa Land! In the eyes of Brooklyn fans, O'Malley joined Adolf Hitler and Joseph Stalin as the three most hated men of the 20th Century.

The poems in the October Trilogy written in the Villanelle form reflect the reaction to these events through the eyes, heart, and mind of a Brooklyn Boy as he travels from age eight to age 14.

October 1951

A child's dream dies on Coogan's Bluff,
He is a Giant hero, this Flying Scot,
Who turns my hopes to a wispy puff.

Why can't I be made of sterner stuff,
To endure my unwelcome lot,
A child's dream dies on Coogan's Bluff.

Before this day, the faithful took no guff,
Those oppose us we know will rot,
Who turns my hopes to a wispy puff.

Dem Bums we worship play strong and tough,
Their story contorted by this historic shot,
A child's dream dies on Coogan's Bluff.

Accept this fate no matter how rough,
Curdling blood that cannot clot,
Who turns my hopes to a wispy puff.

Say no more, I've heard enough,
Only tell me how, why, and what,
A child's dream dies on Coogan's Bluff,
Who turns my hopes to a wispy puff.

October 1955

The Series is knotted three and three,
Today the decisive game,
All on the line for all to see.

Let the joyful throng include me,
When heroes dance with fame,
The Series is knotted three and three.

From years of heartbreak set us free,
No longer consumed by flame,
All on the line for all to see.

Tension surpasses the nth degree,
Fortune is indeed a fickle dame,
The Series is knotted three and three.

End this frustration, I plead of thee,
This time the outcome not the same,
All on the line for all to see.

Send the victory sign, a two-fingered V,
No reason at last to place any blame,
The Series is knotted three and three,
All on the line for all to see.

OCTOBER 1957

Off to L.A., banner headlines scream,
A hated owner consumed by greed,
In disbelief we lose our team.

Beloved stars rise to the top as cream,
Their owner sneers haughtily at our need,
Off to L.A., banner headlines scream.

Not reality, but a nightmarish dream,
I fear the truth is what we read,
In disbelief we lose our team.

Anger justifiable, we blow off steam,
At the perpetrator of this blasphemous deed,
Off to L.A., banner headlines scream.

Victims of a diabolical scheme,
Our prayers and pleas he will not heed,
In disbelief we lose our team.

Betrayal, I fear, is this story's theme,
A poisonous plot from a mutant seed,
Off to L.A., banner headlines scream,
In disbelief we lose our team.

ME AND BOBBY V

Thinking out loud about my first baseball glove
a weathered friend I grew to protect and love,
a model signed by Detroit's Bobby Veach,
sharing unnumbered flannels with the Georgia Peach.

Cobb in center, Wahoo Sam in right, Bobby in left,
When Heilmann arrived, a teammate agile and deft,
Cooperstown's shrine denied for Veach's flames
burned less bright than the game's greatest names.

Bobby's career average stood at three ten,
runs batted in, doubles, and triples -- among best of all men,
in nineteen nineteen, batting a lofty three fifty-five,
There is no tape, you had to see him live.

Scuffed sphere thwacked into cracked leather pocket
echoing the thud of a Fourth of July rocket,
My Bobby's skin nourished by an unlikely oil
me rubbing, caressing, sweating through the toil.

This glove a stranger to a miscue or error,
polishing my credentials as a defensive terror
on fields of pebbly dirt and schoolyard concrete
so many summer days until worn out and beat.

After games in the hundreds this friend fell apart
bringing tears to my eyes and breaking my heart,
I bought a new mitt whose name I cannot recall,
someone anonymously backhanding the ball.

Like Briggs and Ebbets, Crosley, Shibe, Polo Grounds
all forgotten diamonds making history's rounds
Old Bob is remembered by a few baseball fanatics
hooked on the game like compulsive drug addicts.

Bobby V later joined Senators, Red Sox, Yanks,
for his exploits and his glove I can only say thanks
yet I cannot end now before admitting the truth,
thoughts of Bobby V resurrected days of my youth.

NOTIONS OF LOVE

BIRD OF LIGHT

Blackbird rests
on a solitary wire,
now soaring alone,
higher yet higher.
Descending near
on powerful wings,
favoring me with song
so sweetly she sings.
Though ebon in color,
black as night,
her mystical power
turns dark into light.
I know her by name,
in a language Romance,
for all of our time
pray together we dance.

Now This Time

His chance slipped away a time ago,
not again, he silently vows,
listening to her lingering fears,
ageless doubts, missteps, unwise choices,
finally a fragile triumph looking over
its shoulder at what was, what might
    have been.

Please, he pleads inwardly,
look forward to what
    might be.

He is not easily discarded,
nor like others will he flee
    from responsibility,
leaving her stranded in a
    swirling sea,
whose waves toss dreams
one way, then another.

He wears simple garb,
speaking simple words,
standing on solid ground,
not astride a sinewy
    silvery steed.

Trust me at your side,
    he asks,

not to rescue her from
    blackness, but
lighting a way beyond shadow,
so strength may vanquish hurt.

Into the Essence

Peer into my eyes,
take my hand,
give me your trust,
travel with me
not by plane, train,
car, ship, any
mechanical toy.

Come, via our hearts,
to an inner essence
on paths we often walk,
each time taking more steps,
delving deeper into mystery
not shrouded in darkness
or fear of where we go,
what we uncover.

This way is suffused
by love's beacon light,
shining upon discoveries
of what defines us,
allows you to be you,
allows me to be me,
within our sacred togetherness.

Lucky Stars

Walking under an ebony sky
sprinkled with flecks of twinkling light.
Are these my lucky stars
I thank for you?

What did I know of stars?
Occasional nods
to them in song or story,
little more than a fleeting interest.

Came our first night, our first walk,
anon these silvery guides help
navigate life's labyrinth
to discover each in the other.

COME TO MY DREAMS

Guardian of the Night.
keeper of the dark,
I ask a favor.
Take her hand,
calm her fears,
lead her gently
to the depths
of my subconscious
where dreams dwell
so she and I lie together
in sweet embrace,
touching, kissing
till no longer apart.

WISHES FOR YOU

Wade in waters of summer seas
Stroll autumn trails strewn with gifts
from aspens, maples, cottonwoods
Sparkle as crystals
encased in wintry snowflakes
Dance with daffodils
to songs of spring's renewal
Revel in Nature's creation
this day and all.

IMAGINE

Love enveloped by each sheltering fold,
Locked together in warming embrace,
Imagining adventures yet untold

No diamonds, no silver, no purest gold,
Of material riches, desire not a trace,
Love enveloped by each sheltering fold.

Star-studded skies created to behold,
A steady journey, not a rapidly run race,
Imagining adventures yet untold.

Protected from ravages of storm and cold,
Upon me shines radiance of your face,
Love enveloped by each sheltering fold.

Never doubting actions if brash or bold,
Still living days at a measured pace,
Imagining adventures yet untold.

Our shared times never stale or old,
Memories safe in the mind's sacred place,
Love enveloped by each sheltering fold,
Imagining adventures yet untold.

LOVING THAT WALK

I love to watch you walk.
Striding purposefully on sandy stretches
alongside the ditch or on dirt
packed hard by too much sun,
too little rain.
All the while deftly
dodging heaps of horse dung
or mysterious traces of scat
you identify as coyote.

I love to watch you walk.
Not walk, but sashay
from room to room,
your hips moving to and fro,
port, starboard,
swaying to the East, then West.

I love to watch you walk.
Let my hands
find your hips, feel you move,
before gliding along your body,
thinking of snuggling, cuddling,
bundling — whatever the delight.
Oh, but I digress —
We were discussing walking, yes?

I love to watch you walk.
Off with shoes, feet clad
in Elvis socks or perhaps
a flock of flamingos.

Not really walking, but prancing
when you are silly and girlish,
when I want to gently poke
index fingers into your ribs
hearing you giggle as
you squirm from my touch.

BALANCING ACT

Relationships — a daring high wire act,
Doubly dangerous with no safety net,
Playing with fiction, yet living in fact.

Explosive words spoken with little tact,
Much to remember, no chance to forget,
Relationships — a daring high wire act.

Praying our wounded hearts remain intact,
Along this journey not a single regret
Playing with fiction, yet living in fact.

With angels, with devils sign a tenuous pact,
Future times beckoning an unwise bet,
Relationships — a daring high wire act.

Nights of anguish, desired endings inexact,
Two worlds in flux, impossible to set,
Playing with fiction, yet living in fact.

Floods of failings and faults fail to detract,
No abundance of weaknesses to fret,
Relationships — a daring high wire act,
Playing with fiction, yet living in fact.

My Beans

She was damn good looking, smart, liked to laugh a lot, and when she flashed those baby blues — well, I just melted. Her voice dropped an octave when she said "good night" on the phone and you'd swear you were talking to Bacall. Quirky? Yeah, but that was one of her many endearing qualities. Her name meant blackbird in Old French of all languages— maybe even New French for all I knew. Interesting, I suppose, if you like dead languages. The case wasn't exactly the Maltese Falcon. But at 200 bucks a day and expenses, who's quibbling. Besides, I needed the dough. Then she steered me into neighborhoods where I wish I had a platoon of Marines with me. I made a mental note to mention that to her. Our paths crossed years ago, right before Uncle Sam gave me a 12-month paid vacation to Southeast Asia. I considered it the first year of graduate school. Since she and I ran into each other a few months ago, the same old question gnawed at me again. Where did she live when we met on those humid Baltimore nights in August 1967 — a time the hippies called the Summer of Love?

My search took me to the Maryland Room of the Main Library. A woman who reminded me of my third grade teacher made my day. She hauled out a stack of torn and tattered phone books. I bracketed the August 1967 time between the December 1966 and December 1967 directories. "Eureka, I found it!" I could of kissed the librarian, but I didn't want her going into cardiac arrest on my watch. After all, I'm cute and exotic, or so I'm told. My destination was 15 minutes away. I parked my jalopy, got out, and took a few pictures of 2723 North Charles Street. People stared at me. I didn't care. I was just an average Joe looking for one of life's answers. Sure, maybe what I found didn't amount to a hill of beans in this crazy world.

But it was my hill and my beans.

(I am a fan of film noir, and wrote this largely non-fiction prose poem, paying homage to Dashiell Hammett and Raymond Chandler.)

Day in Motion

In darkened stillness,
lay to me near,
hear a poet's words,
strong, yet tenderly clear.

Eyes awaken to light
when song greets morning,
gently, quietly tell
of day's expected dawning.

Sunlit journey done by half,
clouds mingle with blue,
mysteries seek elusive answers
from a hidden telltale clue.

Circles completed at dusk,
anointing an ivory glow
splashed by galactic glitter,
affirming all we know.

Dark stillness once more,
worlds stunningly surreal
with mystical presence,
promising more to reveal.

4 JULY 4TH

Move over America, sorry but you're
in the back seat playing second fiddle,
today I share my fourth of her milestones,
I've lots of catching up to do.

Wide eyes wonder at your fireworks,
yet we ignite our own,
march in private parades,
hearts exchanging salutes.

Remembering our Declarations,
independent bodies
orbiting in tandem around
convergent selves.

Let others run up Old Glory,
we exult in the new,
created mutually, happily free,
embracing life's liberty.

UNLIKELIES

When rivers flow backward,
and mountains grow downward,
When roosters crow at dusk,
and owls awaken at dawn,

When the moon is never full,
and stars never shine,
When armadillos fly, and blue birds swim,
and donkeys howl and coyotes bray,

When kings bow to peasants,
and lions cede their throne,
When airplanes run on pickle juice,
and diamonds lose their luster,

When fires resemble icicles,
and ice cubes turn to ash,
When deserts become oceans,
and camels float out to sea,

When no one reads Shakespeare
and man abandons war.

When these unlikelies happen,
if impossibles come true,
only in such imaginary moments
shall I not treasure you.

A LA CARTE

"The" Sandwich

Rye bread, two slices
crusted with mahogany,
flecked with caraway
  seeds,
spread with grainy,
  yellow mustard,
hosting silvery-skinned,
  oily sardines,
a purple ringlet of onion,
Swiss cheese, nutty
  and dense.

Unseen and unmade,
the gauntlet untaken,
only I accept the dare.

CRISPY, CRUNCHY...GONE

Don't look for the potato chips,
    I ate them,
ate them all, every bless-ed
    son of a spud,
ate them with roast beef,
    rare and red
partnered with the yellow of
    pinon garlic mustard
spread on multigrain rounds
    red and yellow — colors
of New Mexico's flag
    and banners
unfurled in Spain and Sicily,
Macedonia and Montenegro,
by ancient enemies China and Vietnam,
    in Kyrgyzstan, too.

Yes, I ate the potato chips,
low-salt baked chips you bought
    four days ago or
two days you insisted,
sixty percent less salt,
thank goodness not no salt
for taste receptors of
    my tongue
leap at briny sensations,
seasoned temptations.

Yes, I ate the potato chips,
not at once, but over a few days,

each fresh chip crisp as a newly
    printed sawbuck,
crunchy like crinkly paper.
Yes, I ate them all and
yes, they were really good and
yes, I remembered to put
    a rubber band
around the bag so the chips
stayed fresh and crispy
    and crunchy.

UNDELIVERED MERCHANDISE

Maybe the Raven Lunatic tee-shirt
spanning pectorals, stretching across deltoids,
encircling biceps and triceps
caught her attention.
Or maybe the trimmer hips
encased in Slim-Fit jeans
or the tousled, slightly unkempt hair
with brown thatches streaked by a silvery vein
diverted her gaze from the half-filled
glass of red sitting on Farina's bar.
And then there's the age thing —
I'm — let's say older than she might think.
I pegged her for about 40, sculpted eyebrows,
ebony hair borrowed from Anjelica Huston circa 1994.

I swap my credit card
for vegetable chunks, spice-laden garlicky rounds
sunk into cheesy, doughy crust.
"Planning to eat that alone?"
Whoa — an invitation to her dance?
I bite my lower lip, tilt my head
maybe 15 degrees, throw her
you know whose "I Feel Your Pain" look.
"Matter of fact, I've got a dinner partner.
Breakfast and lunch partner, too."
Her eyes round-trip back to the glass of red.
Another night at the end of the bar.

Joe

A cuppa joe, java, coffee,
hot, black, strong.
Cappuccinos, espressos, lattes —
skip the fancy concoctions created by someone striving
for the exalted title of barista, turning levers,
twisting handles, making enough steam to power
a moderately-sized seagoing vessel.
How about a decaf? Why bother?
A coffee-lover's shirt blares "Bad coffee sucks!"
Profound.
Pour me coffee slightly less thick than 10W30 motor oil.
Turkish coffee, so dense a spoon stands upright -
a silver obelisk in a black pool.
How many cups a day?
Depends on what you read, who you ask.
Might send my blood pressure out of range...Bad.
Might reduce my chances of pancreatic cancer...Good.
You pay your money, you take your chances.

The Lobster Trap

How lucky that prized crustacean
so plentiful and cheap, letting us
sustain ourselves on lobster rolls
those months on the Cape.

An assembly line of lobster rolls,
only occasionally interrupted
by grilled cheese sandwiches
at the Falmouth Friendly's.

Tucked between halves of pedestrian
hot dog buns, lobster meat creamy
with mayonnaise, flecked with pimento
and pickle, reminding me
of emerald eyes, red hair, pale skin
speckled with freckles I liked but you did not.

How lucky we were,
lobsters forever available
or so I thought until
their attraction dimmed
when the season ended
one June afternoon.

COFFEE HOUR

We meet for coffee. A blind date
but not exactly. Call this a pre-date
that might spawn a future date.
Lunch. Dinner. Dinner and a movie
leading to ... slow down.
I'm not comfortable, it's been a while,
too soon for involvement, even casual,
let alone commitment. Whoa there, fella.
My friends tell me I need to get back in the game,
rejoin the hunt.
She's two years out of school, me five...
older not necessarily wiser.
She shares a place with two roommates,
I live alone now. Alone, but not lonely,
I tell myself every day.
She runs, meditates, does yoga.
I'm a gym rat. Don't mention my tattoos.
Where is this small talk going?
She likes ballet, chamber music, tennis.
Jazz, rock, baseball, football for me.
Ever been to a hockey game? I ask.
No.
She's into a career, thinking about law school.
I'm, uh, shall we say still finding myself.
She reads poetry. I prefer Spenser,
the Boston detective, not the English poet.
Did she roll her eyes?
Bergman, Fellini, Truffaut her movie faves,
Bogart, Hitchcock, Woody mine.
She's pretty enough.

Not flashy, thank goodness,
certainly not plain.
I like the eyes — soft brown —
goes well with ash blonde hair,
not quite shoulder length.
Don't want to stare.
More coffee? I ask.
Maybe another half cup.
Good sign or just politeness?
Not much in common, I guess,
but I feel comfortable with her.
Opposites attract, maybe.
"I really have to go," she says.
Summoning my resolve,
I take the hand she offers.
"Call you sometime?" I say.
Her lips move — not the expected "I don't think so."
Instead my brain registers, "Yes, I'd like that."

ODE TO CHEESE

Let me say proudly
if I may please,
I proclaim my love
for all sorts of cheese.
Lord knows their number,
so many kinds,
some with,
some sans rinds.

Add basil and spinach
to fresh mozzarella,
hear me sing like
a most happy fella.
On a simple salad
go heavy with the bleu,
adds a crumbly touch,
so very good, who knew?
Almost always expensive
any brand of brie,
guess I can afford some
but wish it were free.

Before I sleep at night
I always say a prayer
that the very next day
I'll find good gruyere.
And though it be holey
I would be remiss
if I added ham to rye bread
but omitted the Swiss.

My politics are personal,
but of cheese I'm a partisan,
especially when grating
a wedge of aged Parmesan.
Each and every Greek salad
would taste even greater
with the healthy addition
of snowy white feta.

When fixing macaroni
nothing could be better
than a 10-ounce stick
of extra sharp cheddar.
Easy for me to say
I woulda, I coulda
stopped by the cheese case
for a slab of Dutch gouda.

Made from fresh milk
of sheep, cow, or goat,
all of these cheeses
cause me to emote.
I'm not at all shy
about paying homage
to what the French
exclaim as le belle fromage.

This food is so blessed
I even believe Jesus
turned water into wine
to accompany his cheeses.

ARIA FOR ARBORIO

The risotto does not sing,
she complained; put batteries
in your hearing aids, be still,
then listen, he replied.

RANDOM SAMPLES I

INTO YOUR DARK

Erebus carries you
from light into her
dark realm where
cynical demons stir
cauldrons of spite.

Sip from the chalice
of Incubus, the evil drink
seeping into your veins,
corroding the soul,
purging lingering vestiges
of good from your heart.

Slip deeper into fog,
turn away from offerings
of solace and compassion,
stain their intentions with words
steeped in venom.

An insidious disease
defies diagnosis, yet
reveals truths with
ultimate clarity.

KILLING GROUND

This place we call home
now a bloody killing ground,
no longer merely alarming,
death and destruction abound.

Malls, churches, shops, theaters,
schools of every grade,
when will those in power,
end their masquerade?

How many more innocents
must lie uneasy in their grave
before we rise and say enough,
counted among the brave?

Another question left to ask
is one we've asked before,
when does this nightmare end,
and today we ask it once more.

REVOLUTION?

They appear out of nowhere,
slogans scrawled on every wall,
down with this, down with that
down with just about all.

Angry voices against everything,
but what do they defend?
Are they authentic rebels
or merely playing pretend?

Hear their call for change,
igniting a revolution,
perhaps only making noise,
not a process of evolution.

You cannot be for nothing,
far better a righteous cause,
breaking down barriers,
overturning oppressive laws.

MORNING

Mourning doves solemnly coo
a preamble to parking lot crunches
heralding delivery of
this day's news, the same daily news
as yesterday and the day before
and the day to come, I bet.
Death, destruction, maltreatment,
malfeasance, abuse, aggression,
arrogance, unwarranted incursions,
ill-advised excursions, incessant
drum beats of despair.

Find Albuquerque sharing
Latitude 35.05 with
Chattanooga, Tennessee;
Gundagai, Australia;
Nicosia, Cyprus.
At longitude 106.39,
Saskatoon, Canada,
Ciudad Juarez, Mexico,
join the Duke City.

And their news?
Drug-trafficking gangs attack
Southern civility in the shadow
of Lookout Mountain;
Aussies tolerate aborigines,
yet send Middle Eastern
asylum seekers to Cambodia;
Turks and Greeks forever squabbling

in Cyprus. What, you think they're
chatting amiably while sampling
tumblers of ouzo and arak?
Crime, high HIV rates cloud
the prairie, but Canadians seem too
damn polite to discuss such unpleasantries.
Juarez? we know that script.

And that's the news.

CIRCLING THE SQUARE

My partner and I are lost in the City by the Bay,
not **The City**...but Oakland,
Gertrude Stein's "there is no there there,"
Civic boosters now proclaim Oakland
"the place where it's at".... who can say?

Still the city of the fall-short-again
Athletics of the baseball world;
where hapless and woeful are among adjectives
applied to football's hapless and woeful Raiders;
where freeways honor architects of long ago victories,
where the Coast Starlight, California Zephyr,
and freight cars carrying invisible cargoes
rumble down the Embarcadero, the spine
of Jack London Square — the place we can't find..

Sorry.
Somewhere I got lost talking
about how we got lost.

We drive into one-of-those-on-every-corner
gas station-minimart combos, where a smiling
but equally lost Chinese girl suggests
asking folks filling up at the pumps.
"She knows directions," a shaved-head black dude
tells me, pointing to a woman of undetermined age,
his mom, or grandmother, or aunt.
Dreadlocks frame a face brimming with warm cocoa,
perfectly cast for a funky movie set in Savannah

or New Orleans, or lingering on the
pages of Carl Hiaasen's latest.

"Jack London Square?"
Her eyes seem deep in thought, perhaps
searching for messages from hidden cartographers.
"Okay, take a right out of here, go right on Webster,
through the Alameda Tunnel in the right lane, then........"
I listen intently, hoping her words register
on my internal GPS. I've got it....
right, right, right, the tunnel...
A troika of hugs, mutual God blesses,
deliverance of thanks.
We're on our way. We are not.
Our guardian angel waves us to a halt.
"Follow us, when we pull away at Jackson Street,
you keep going and you'll hit the square."
Blessings bestowed again.
Thirty minutes later we find the square
and our hotel for the next two nights,
thanks to our unnamed benefactor

Gertrude Stein, meet the Black Madonna,
the "there," of this City by the Bay.

At the Airport

Watching everyone parade,
for some it's the real thing,
for others only a charade,
they kiss, they hug, hello or goodbye,
too many others don't know why.

ON THE TRAIL

When night falls on the Pecos
and the cattle seem asleep,
you can find this tired old cowboy
in slumber long and deep.

Hours of eating trail dust,
miles of riding drag,
little comfort in the saddle
astride my old and weary nag.

Sitting in the fire light,
with one more can of beans,
drinking bitter coffee again,
wearing torn and tattered jeans.

Watching close the midnight sky,
afraid it might spit lightning,
nothing worse than a stampeding herd,
nothing so deadly or frightening.

Remember when Clint rode the range,
a Friday fixture, as Rowdy Yates,
Here's me — still rounding up strays,
and him — products of our fates.

Untitled

In deepest sanctuaries
a will to conspire
seemingly impossible schemes
created to realize
otherwise implausible dreams
where uncounted thrills
send us careening
toward unfortunate spills
and non-sensical delights
are residuals of
non-refundable nights.

Random Samples II

HUG-O-MANIA

My eye's corner glimpses a familiar mug,
soon we stand face-to-face,
searching for the proper embrace,
and as if by silent assent, we choose hug.

Handshakes seem out of date,
the firm, solid grips of yore
when strength oozed from every pore,
a measure of man's character trait.

And when a woman offered a hand,
we accepted with a gentle grasp,
whispering enchantment as we clasp,
such niceties now in scant demand.

Invoking optional pats on the back,
arms wrapped around our necks,
not complete kisses but polite pecks,
finding places on a warm, fuzzy track.

Running into a long ago flame,
remembered cheeks lightly brush,
now neither feeling the slightest rush,
for both know nothing is the same.

So when we seek to sincerely endear,
choose not the cold shoulder shrug,
instead the warming mutual hug
bringing us to places so near.

Homage to Dr. Williams

So much depends
  upon
this clunky
  Ford
needing a tank
  of gas
in a gravel
  driveway

DISAPPEARANCE

I'd be as sly
as the slyest fox
if I could solve
the mystery of my socks.
They emerge from the washer
so fresh and so clean
black, blue, and brown,
an occasional green.
I am not especially confident
yet I manage some smiles
when I gaze at solids,
plaids, and even argyles.
Into the dryer
purged of all lint
my socks disappear
without the slightest hint.
I've checked lost and found
posted alerts
all the while thankful
I've not lost my shirts.
Despite the sock mystery
my feet won't go bare
for a fistful of dollars
I'll have a new pair.

Sir *

New York City's former mayor
named a knight of the realm,
Sir Michael Bloomberg, Sir Mike to his pals.
Make that Sir Mike with an asterisk,
this knighthood is honorary.

Am I about to join Sir Mike
at some imaginary Round Table
in a make-believe Camelot?

Reaching shores of a certain decade
whose number I shall not divulge
bestows upon me the honorific of sir —
at least lots of folks believe so.

"Did you find everything, sir?"
asks the Whole Foods cashier.
"How's the salmon taste tonight, sir?"
wonders Justin, my obedient server.
"I hope you enjoy the movie, sir,"
offers the teen-aged ticket ripper.

A proletarian friend likes to reply,
"Don't call me sir, I work for a living."
I cannot say that —
I don't work, at least not for a living.

Has my memory lapsed upon entry
into this hallowed time?
I remember no investiture

into the ranks of knighthood,
no dubbing of my shoulders
with anyone's sovereign sword,
no choosing of armor,
or lance, or mace and chain;
I wield no broadsword,
no squire serves me,
no jousts on my schedule.
Yet I am sir, so I go with the flow;
Sir Mark, if you please,
with or without an asterisk.

LOST AND POUND

The eccentric Ezra Pound
buried six feet underground,
though he is lost
we'll make do with Frost.

RERUNS

Too many reruns playing in theaters
      of the mind
not at the budget movie, admission
      far too steep,
lay your money down now, free passes
      not valid this performance
ticket torn for a script read long
      before,
groping about in the dark
      for a seat
always room for one
      more.

That Other Piper

The pie-eyed Piper
marches to the beat
of a diffident drummer.
Reeling from discordant notes,
kneeling from the weight,
concealing realities,
revealing absurdities.

The pie-eyed Piper
marches to the beat
of a diffident drummer.
Fearing unlit tomorrows,
tearing at frightful todays,
hearing alien voices,
veering to naked choices

The pie-eyed Piper
marches to the beat
of a diffident drummer.
Slinking into shadows,
thinking not of exits,
sinking always deeper,
winking at the reaper.

The pie-eyed Piper
marches to the beat
of a diffident drummer.
Sizing up options,
mobilizing final choices,
energizing hidden clarities,
rising with unexpected rarities.

THE HORNET AND ITCH

You are a bug, she said
    matter-of-factly,
implying he is some creepy,
crawly, flying, buzzing specimen
    who bugs, annoys, irks
baffles, puzzles, perplexes her.

Next question: What bug would
    you be?
He thought what creepy,
crawly, flying, buzzing specimen
    he'd choose.
A hornet, he exclaimed.
Why? Don't really know.

What sort of bug would
    you be?
Hmmmm....an itch.
An itch? That's not a bug,
it's what you do if a
creepy, crawly, flying, buzzing
    specimen
bit you, stung you, or landed on
    your delicate flesh.

Would that create a rash to be
    itched?
Most certainly a rash.
    A rash! Oh, mon!

Great Japanese movie,
Kurosawa the director.
What's next? Japanese beetles.
Sayonara.

EPILOGUE

What's In a Name

Man, what am I doing here
Away from a classroom for how many years?
Running headlong into a whole new world
Killing myself with doubt

Finding a new outlet for expression
Learning what I never knew
Emerging from darkness
Into the bright light of ideas
Surprising myself every day
Hearing my words spewing out
Elegantly, noisily, passionately
Rewarding myself when it sounds right

About the Author

Mark Fleisher was born on Cinco de Mayo, 1943, in Brooklyn, New York. He graduated from Erasmus Hall High School in Brooklyn and received a Bachelor of Science in Journalism from Ohio University. He is an Air Force veteran, serving in Vietnam as a combat news reporter. After a 22-year newspaper career, he worked in Chemung (NY) County government as director of public information and as a veterans' counselor.

His freelance writing has appeared in Life in the Finger Lakes magazine, the New York State Historical Journal, Black Athlete Sports Network, and upstate New York newspapers. He is a contributor to the 2015 Fixed and Free Poetry Anthology. He moved to Albuquerque in October 2013 from the Finger Lakes area of New York.